The Ukrainian Crisis and European Security

Implications for the United States and U.S. Army

F. Stephen Larrabee, Peter A. Wilson, John Gordon IV

Prepared for the United States Army

For more information on this publication, visit www.rand.org/t/rr903

Library of Congress Control Number: 2015939208

ISBN 978-0-8330-8834-5

Published by the RAND Corporation, Santa Monica, Calif.

© Copyright 2015 RAND Corporation

RAND® is a registered trademark.

Preface

This report, part of an exploratory series for the U.S. Army, is a think piece about the strategic implications of the ongoing Ukraine-Russia crisis for the Department of the Army. This analysis provides a first look at some of the broader strategic implications for the U.S. Army of the Ukrainian crisis. The report is intended to be of interest to the military and civilian leadership within the Department of the Army.

This research was sponsored by the Department of the Army and conducted within the RAND Arroyo Center's Strategy and Resources Program. RAND Arroyo Center, part of the RAND Corporation, is a federally funded research and development center sponsored by the United States Army.

The Project Unique Identification Code (PUIC) for the project that produced this document is HQD146843.

Contents

Summary

Vladimir Putin's decision to annex Crimea and to destabilize eastern Ukraine has sparked widespread concern among Western policymakers that Russia has embarked on a more confrontational policy that could have far-reaching implications for Russia's relations with the West and for European stability. The annexation of Crimea challenges two basic assumptions on which U.S. policy toward Europe in the post–Cold War era has been based: (1) that Europe is essentially stable and secure, thereby freeing the United States to focus greater attention on other areas, particularly Asia and the Middle East, and (2) that Russia had become more of a partner than an adversary.

The annexation of Crimea suggests that both these assumptions need to be revisited. Europe has returned front and center on the U.S. policy agenda. This means that the United States will have to find a new balance among competing priorities in Europe, the Middle East, and Asia. After the annexation of Crimea and the military effort to destabilize eastern Ukraine, Russia can hardly be viewed as a partner. The United States will thus have to reexamine the basic premises on which its Russian policy is based as it seeks to adjust to dealing with a more nationalistic and assertive Russia.

This report will present the major events and circumstances surrounding the Ukrainian crisis and briefly discuss their importance, then conclude with observations on the possible implications for the U.S. Army. This report does not present concrete recommendations for action, but rather considerations for those charged with planning the size, posture, and composition of the Army.

Ukraine's Strategic Importance for Russia

At its core, the current crisis in Ukraine is about Ukraine's future strategic orientation—whether Kiev will be allowed to choose its own independent foreign policy or be compelled to remain within the Russian sphere of influence. Ukraine's future orientation will also influence Russia's long-term geostrategic orientation and political path. Without Ukraine, as Zbigniew Brzezinski has pointed out, Russia ceases to be a Eurasian empire. However, if Moscow regains control over Ukraine, Russia automatically again regains the wherewithal to become an imperial state, spanning Europe and Asia.

In addition, Ukraine poses an important potential political-ideological threat to Putin's model of authoritarian state capitalism. A stable, independent, democratically oriented Ukraine on Russia's western border with close ties to Europe and the West represents an attractive alternative model to Putin's attempt to establish "managed democracy" in Russia and the rest of the post-Soviet space. From Putin's point of view, the real danger is *contagion*—that Russian citizens might begin to agitate for a similar, more open system in Russia. Putin has sought to weaken and discredit the government in Kiev, portraying it as composed of "fascists" and "neo-Nazis."

Reassuring Eastern Europe

The Russian annexation of Crimea and the attempt to destabilize eastern Ukraine have made Poland and the Baltic countries very nervous and prompted calls for NATO to station combat forces in Eastern Europe and the Baltic states. Against the background of this increasing clamor for additional troops, NATO approved plans for the creation of a 4,000-man rapid reaction force. Plans call for a portion of this force to have an essentially permanent presence in Eastern Europe, with the remainder of the force able to be dispatched to trouble spots in the region within 48 hours. This upgraded force is intended to be the spearhead of a much larger rapid reaction force designed to enhance

NATO's ability to effectively carry out crisis management missions in regions far from NATO members' capitals.

Strengthening the Security of the Baltic States

The question of how to ensure the security of the Baltic states also has emerged as a critical security issue in the debate. President Putin's annexation of Crimea and covert and overt attempt to destabilize eastern Ukraine have generated fears in the Baltic states that Russia could take steps designed to weaken their independence and territorial integrity. While an overt Russian attack against the Baltic states is highly unlikely, there are reasons for concern, given Putin's emphasis on Russia's responsibility to defend the rights of the Russian minority abroad. Thus, in the aftermath of the annexation of Crimea and Russia's attempt to destabilize eastern Ukraine by overt military means, greater attention needs to be focused on enhancing the security of the Baltic states.

A New Model in Russian Military Thinking

In addition, Russia's military actions in Crimea and in the Ukrainian crisis demonstrated a new model of Russian military thinking, combining traditional instruments of Russian military thought with a new emphasis on surprise, deception, and strategic ambiguity. This model enables Russia to disguise its real intentions and conduct an "invasion by stealth." Countries such as the Baltic states and Moldova, which are on Russia's periphery and home to large ethnic Russian minorities, are worried that they could be the targets of this new Russian approach to warfare. In the future, NATO is likely to face Russian aggression that relies on approaches and techniques associated with Russia's low-cost annexation of Crimea and the destabilization of eastern Ukraine.

New Uncertainties in the Black Sea Region

The annexation of Crimea has shifted the military balance in the Black Sea region more strongly in Russia's favor and significantly increased Russia's strategic footprint in the region. The expansion of the Black Sea Fleet will strengthen Russia's ability to project power in the region and raises important questions about how Russia will use that power. Many Western officials worry that Moldova could come under increasing pressure if Putin is successful in destabilizing eastern Ukraine.

Putin's Increasing Commitment to the Pro-Russian Separatists

Since the downing of the MH17 commercial airliner in July 2014, Russia has increased weapon deliveries to the pro-Russian rebels, as well as the firepower of those weapons. This military support and direct engagement in the conflict has succeeded in turning the military tide of the battle in the separatists' favor—and raised the pressure on President Petro Poroshenko to agree to a fragile cease-fire that leaves two key cities, Donetsk and Luhansk, in the hands of the "rebel" forces.

Implications for the U.S. Army

The Ukrainian crisis has three key implications for the U.S. Army. First, the assumption by the U.S. national security leadership that Europe had become a strategically quiet zone in Eurasia and that the United States could shift its attention to other regions, especially Asia and the Middle East, has been overturned. Europe will play a more important role in U.S. national security strategy in the coming decade, not a lesser one.

Second, if NATO now has to build a much more robust deterrence and defense posture in Eastern Europe, the Army and Air Force will need to revisit their planning assumptions, which have minimized

U.S. military commitments to that region since the end of the Cold War.

Third, when added to the steady or growing demands for U.S. military deployments and activities elsewhere (e.g., East Asia, the Middle East, Africa), the more uncertain security environment in Europe argues for a reappraisal of the balance between the requirements of U.S. defense strategy and the resources available to support it. Put simply, many elements of the joint force are being stretched thin through attempts to meet new commitments that were not foreseen even as recently as January 2014, when the Quadrennial Defense Review completed its work and the FY 2015 budget submission went forward.

Finally, it is important to note that several of the considerations put forward in this report, such as increasing the U.S. military's posture in Europe, involve political risks that are beyond the scope of this document to address. Furthermore, we offer no judgment on the wisdom of increased investments in defense to address the increased uncertainty and risk in Europe in the context of the overall U.S. fiscal situation for similar reasons. Rather, we note that the status quo that existed when the most recent defense strategy documents were produced has changed, and therefore a reexamination of commitments, both in terms of forces in Europe and defense outlays, is in order.

Acknowledgments

The authors would like to express their thanks to RAND colleague Terry Kelley and to our peer reviewers, James Dobbins, Robert Nurick (of the Atlantic Council), and David Ochmanek, for their helpful comments on an earlier draft of this manuscript.

Abbreviations

A&D	aerospace and defense
EU	European Union
GDP	gross domestic product
MAP	Membership Action Plan
NATO	North Atlantic Treaty Organization
PfP	Partnership for Peace
SAM	surface-to-air missile

CHAPTER ONE

Introduction

Vladimir Putin's decision to annex Crimea and to destabilize eastern Ukraine has sparked widespread concern among Western policymakers that Russia has embarked on a more confrontational policy that could have far-reaching implications for Russia's relations with the West and for European stability.

The annexation of Crimea challenges two basic assumptions on which U.S. policy toward Europe in the post–Cold War era has been based: (1) that Europe is essentially stable and secure, thereby freeing the United States to focus greater attention on other areas, particularly Asia and the Middle East, and (2) that Russia had become more of a partner than an adversary. The annexation of Crimea suggests that both these assumptions need to be revisited. Europe has returned front and center on the U.S policy agenda, and Russia can hardly be considered an ally, having blatantly violated one of the basic principles established by the Helsinki Final Act in 1975—that European borders shall not be changed by force.

This report examines the causes and implications of the Ukrainian crisis, which began in November 2013 with Ukrainian President Viktor Yanukovych's decision, taken under strong Russian pressure, not to sign the Ukraine–European Union Association Agreement, and key events and conditions that followed in 2014. It concludes with observations on the possible implications for U.S. policy and the U.S. military, particularly the U.S. Army. This document does not present concrete recommendations for action, but rather considerations for those charged with planning the size, posture, and composition of the Army.

The report is divided into four chapters. Chapter Two examines the geopolitical roots of the Ukrainian crisis, with particular attention to Russian perspectives and policy. Why was Russia so concerned by Ukraine's decision to sign the Ukraine–European Union Association Agreement? What were Russia's key concerns and objections to the agreement? What does this imply for future relations with the West, especially the United States?

Chapter Three discusses the implications for the United States. What impact is the crisis likely to have on U.S. policy? Particular attention is paid to the impact on the EU and its "post-modern" agenda, the future of NATO, and America's role in Europe.

The final chapter focuses on the implications for the U.S. Army. What does the Ukrainian crisis imply for the future role of the Army? What should be its main concerns and priorities in the coming decade? What needs to change? Why? In what way?

CHAPTER TWO

The Geopolitical Roots and Dynamics of the Ukrainian Crisis

At its core, the current crisis is about Ukraine's future strategic orientation—whether Kiev will be allowed to freely choose its own independent foreign policy or will be compelled to remain within Russia's sphere of influence. Ukraine's future orientation will also influence Russia's long-term geostrategic orientation and political path. Without Ukraine, as Zbigniew Brzezinski has pointed out, Russia ceases to be a Eurasian empire.[1] However, if Moscow regains control over Ukraine, Russia automatically regains the wherewithal to become an imperial state, spanning Europe and Asia.

In addition, Ukraine poses an important potential political-ideological threat to Putin's model of authoritarian state capitalism. A stable, independent, democratically oriented Ukraine on Russia's western border with close ties to Europe and the West represents an attractive alternative model to Putin's attempt to establish "managed democracy" in Russia and the rest of the post-Soviet space. From Putin's point of view, the real danger is *contagion*—that Russian citizens might begin to agitate for a similar more open system in Russia. Hence, Putin has sought to weaken and discredit the government in Kiev, portraying it as composed of "fascists" and "neo-Nazis."

Ukraine also has a special importance to Moscow because of its close links to Russia in the defense field. Russia is highly dependent on Ukraine's aerospace and defense (A&D) industry. Approximately

---

[1] Zbigniew Brzezinski, *The Grand Chessboard*, New York: Basic Books, 1997, p. 46.

30 percent of Ukraine's military exports to Russia cannot currently be substituted by Russian domestic production.[2] If Ukraine stops its sale of key subsystems, Russia will have to make costly investments to reproduce these high-technology capabilities to sustain its ambitious modernization programs.

Russia was the third-largest buyer of Ukrainian defense-related products from 2009 to 2013. There are some parts and services that Russia imports only from Ukraine. For example, the Russian military depends heavily on Motor Sich in the southeastern Ukrainian city of Zaporizhia for helicopter engines and on the Antonov plant in Kiev for transport planes.[3] The Southern Machine Building Plant Association (Yuzmash) in Dnipropetrovsk, which designs, manufactures, and services rockets and missiles, is also critically important for the Russian military. More than half of the components of Russia's ground-based intercontinental ballistic missile force come from Ukraine.[4]

Russian officials have downplayed the impact that a severing of defense ties would have on Russia's planned modernization program and the general state of Russian-Ukrainian defense relations. Although Ukrainian exports represent a small fraction—between 2 and 4 percent—of Russia's overall military imports, many branches of the Russian military would suffer without these parts and services. The Russian defense industry would experience a shortage of essential components, and weapon systems integral to Russia's strategic nuclear forces could be compromised without regular Ukrainian servicing.[5]

A severing of defense contracts with Russia would have an even more severe impact on Ukraine and could lead to the collapse of some of Ukraine's defense firms in the southern and eastern parts

---

[2]   See Igor Sutyagin and Michael Clarke, "Ukraine Military Dispositions—the Military Ticks Up While the Clock Ticks Down," RUSI Briefing Paper, April 2014, for a description of the unique dependence the Russia Armed Forces have on high-technology Ukrainian A&D production.

[3]   Alexandra McLees and Eugene Rumer, "Saving Ukraine's Defense Industry," Carnegie Endowment for Peace, July 30, 2014, p. 2.

[4]   McLees and Rumer, 2014, p. 2.

[5]   McLees and Rumer, 2014, p. 2.

of the country, exacerbating economic problems and creating a large pool of unemployed highly skilled nuclear specialists who might be tempted to find employment in rogue states or with other international proliferators.[6]

Additionally, Ukraine is important for the development of Putin's plans to create a Eurasian Union. Without it, the union has little chance of success. Russian concern that Ukraine's conclusion of the Association Agreement with the EU would preclude Kiev from joining the Eurasian Union was an important catalyst for the initiation of the current crisis. President Yanukovych's last-minute refusal—under heavy Russian pressure—to sign the Association Agreement with the EU touched off massive spontaneous protests on the Maidan—the site of the protests that sparked the Orange Revolution and brought President Viktor Yushchenko to power in December 2004.

The increased violence and the attacks by the security forces on the protesters resulted in a precipitous loss of support for Yanukovych within his own Party of Regions. His subsequent ouster in mid-February 2014 set off alarm bells in the Kremlin because it left a highly unstable power vacuum in Ukraine that pro-Western and nationalist forces began to fill. The political upheaval in Ukraine threatened to deal a severe blow to Putin's hope of drawing Ukraine back into the Russian orbit and using the Eurasian Union as a vehicle for increasing Russian influence in the post-Soviet space. A pro-Western Ukraine closely tied to Europe would alter the strategic balance in Central Europe and pose a significant obstacle to Putin's goal of reestablishing Russia as a Eurasian power. It also would increase the possibility of Ukrainian membership in NATO—Russia's strategic nightmare.

---

[6] Helping the Ukraine A&D industries transition toward a more globalized marketplace should be high on any Atlantic Alliance agenda of providing Ukraine with broader financial and economic assistance.

The Annexation of Crimea

Putin's annexation of Crimea caught the United States and its European allies by surprise. However, the swiftness and efficiency with which it was carried out suggests that contingency plans for such an operation had been worked out well in advance. The annexation, from start to finish, took less than two weeks and was accomplished with a minimum of bloodshed and loss of life—a remarkable achievement.

The military seizure of the region was skillfully camouflaged. Russian troops were clandestinely infiltrated into Ukraine in unmarked uniforms. The troops were able to take over Ukrainian barracks and outposts without firing a shot. By the time the West was aware that Crimea was under attack, it was too late to organize an effective military response. Key Ukrainian outposts and installations were already in Russian hands.

The annexation was greatly facilitated by the fact that the Ukrainian armed forces stationed in Crimea were under strict orders from the Ukrainian government not to take military action against the Russian forces, to avoid escalating the violence and provoking a broader and harsher intervention by Russia.

In effect, Crimea represented a new form of "hybrid warfare"—a skillful mixture of overt military measures and covert action, combined with an aggressive use of propaganda and disinformation carefully calculated to avoid crossing established thresholds for military response. By deploying special operation forces in unmarked uniforms, Putin was able to sow enough confusion and doubt to prevent effective countermeasures from being taken.

Public support for the annexation among the ethnic Russian population in Crimea was strong. Ethnic Russians, who make up 60 percent of the peninsula's population, voted overwhelmingly for the incorporation of Crimea into Russia in the referendum held on March 18, 2014. This strong popular support gave the annexation a superficial veneer of international legitimacy.

However, the annexation of Crimea is likely to entail substantial economic and political costs, many of which do not seem to have been considered or well understood at the time the decision to annex

Crimea was made. The annexation has had a negative impact on virtually every aspect of farming in Crimea, from credit to irrigation.[7] Buyers from big international grain firms, such as Cargill and Dreyfus, avoid Crimea because of the Western boycott of its products. In addition, in April 2014 Ukraine shut off the spigot for the main irrigation canal, depriving the peninsula of water essential for many crops. With Ukrainian banks closed, farmers have had trouble getting credit for seed and fertilizer.

The tourist industry, the backbone of Crimea's economy, has also suffered. Tourism in 2014 was down by 30–35 percent. Hotels and restaurants have begun declining credit cards, creating difficulties for many tourists, while major banks fear sanctions and are reluctant to do business in Crimea. Meanwhile, the costs of developing Crimea's economy have continued to mount. Rather than a lucrative tourist attraction, Crimea threatens to become a major drain on the Russian economy.

The popularity of the annexation of Crimea in Russia—and the ease with which it was achieved—may have encouraged Putin to believe that eastern Ukraine could be destabilized via some of the same methods and tactics that were employed in Crimea. However, the political, cultural and demographic situation in eastern Ukraine differs significantly from that in Crimea. The majority of Crimea's population is composed of ethnic Russians who wanted to rejoin Russia. Thus, Putin could count on strong public support for annexing Crimea.

The situation in eastern Ukraine is quite different. The majority of Ukraine's population is composed of ethnic Ukrainians, whose primary language is Russian. They favor close ties to Russia, but they do not want to join Russia or be independent of Ukraine. Thus, Putin could not count on the overwhelming support of the local population as he could in Crimea.

In eastern Ukraine, Russia employed some of the same tactics that it had used in Crimea and in Georgia in 2008. Russia massed troops along the Ukrainian-Russian border and conducted exercises along the

---

[7]   Neal MacFarqhuar, "Aid Elusive, Crimea Farms Face Hurdles," *New York Times*, July 8, 2014.

border. This was a transparent attempt to exert psychological pressure on Ukraine. But it also kept the Russian troops in a state of high readiness in case they actually had to be deployed in combat missions.

The Crash of MH17

The shooting down of a Malaysian commercial airliner, MH17, on July 17, 2014, which resulted in the death of 298 innocent passengers, unexpectedly complicated Putin's game plan of covert intervention. While a final judgment regarding responsibility for the downing of the aircraft will have to await the results of an independent international inquiry, there is strong, perhaps overwhelming, evidence that the plane was shot down by a surface-to-air missile (SAM) fired from separatist territory.[8]

The MH17 incident sparked worldwide moral outrage and focused international attention on Russia's "hidden hand" in the arming, training, and financing of the separatists. The decision to provide the rebel forces with an advanced radar-guided SAM system, the SA-11 (aka BUK-MI), highlights the extent of direct Russian military support for the separatists.

However, rather than acceding to the growing international pressure to halt support for the separatists, Putin decided to up the ante. He stepped up support for the separatists and clandestinely deployed several thousand Russian regular army troops in Ukraine, as well as

---

[8]   According to U.S. Ambassador Samantha Power, speaking at the UN Security Council meeting in New York, an SA-11 missile system, which has the capability of reaching an aircraft flying at 33,000 ft.—the altitude at which the Malaysian aircraft was flying—was spotted in the area of the shoot-down. In addition, separatist officials had boasted on social media of shooting down a plane on the day of the crash, apparently unaware that the target was a civilian airliner. The postings on social media were withdrawn later in the day. See Karen De Young, "U.S.: Plane Was Downed from Rebel-Held Area," *Washington Post,* July 19, 2014. An analysis of the "black boxes" recovered from MA-17 indicates that the aircraft suffered a catastrophic explosive decompression event, consistent with a hit by a high-explosive fragmentation warhead of a high-performance SAM. Also see "MH-17 Crash: Investigation Focuses on '25 Metal Shards,'" BBC NEWS Europe, September 12, 2014, for the results of the Dutch analysis of the shoot down.

dozens of unmarked tanks, armored personnel carriers, missile launchers, and military personnel.[9] It was a bold move that was successful. The massive covert intervention by Russian regular army troops turned the military tide of battle and dealt a fatal blow to the Ukrainian forces, which previously had been on the verge of routing the separatist rebels.

Putin's decision to double down rather than bow to Western pressure provides an important glimpse into his character: Through his determination to maintain the upper hand, he succeeded in changing the political dynamics on the ground and reversing the military tide of battle. His message was clear: Push me and I will push back even harder.

The military intervention was accompanied by important political changes in the separatist leadership. In August, Igor Girkin (aka Strelkov) was replaced as military commander of the Donetsk separatists. A Russian citizen and former member of the Federal Security Service (FSB) (the successor to the KGB), Girkin had fought in Chechnya, Transnistria, and Bosnia and was associated with a number of nationalist causes. His removal was part of a broader shake-up of the separatist leadership, which included the resignation of Alexander Borodai, prime minister of the self-declared Donetsk Peoples Republic. Girkin and Borodai were replaced by little-known Ukrainian officials in an attempt to stress the "Ukrainian" roots of the insurgency and downplay the strong Russian connection.

The Minsk Agreement

The military advances made by the pro-Russian separatists at the end of August 2014, thanks largely to the introduction of regular Russian army units, represented a stunning reversal for the Ukrainian government. With the separatists on the offensive and the Ukrainian forces badly battered and demoralized, President Petro Poroshenko appears

---

[9]   Ukrainian sources estimated that the Russians sent in as many as 10,000 troops, But NATO's estimate of several thousand troops seems more likely. See Roman Olearchyk and Neil Buckley, "Russian Stealth Forced Ukraine into a Ceasefire," *Financial Times*, September 14, 2014.

to have felt that he had little choice but to accept the cease-fire agreement worked out with the separatists in Minsk, the capital of Belarus, on September 5. The 12-point peace plan contained a number of important concessions to the separatists, including an amnesty, special self-governing status for the territories occupied by the separatists, and protections for the Russian language. In addition, it allowed the separatist-controlled regions to elect their own judges, create their own police forces, and develop deeper ties with Russia.[10]

Many Ukrainians fear that the agreement gives too many concessions to the separatists. Poroshenko has defended the agreement, arguing that it contains no concession regarding separatism or Ukraine's territorial integrity. In a narrow sense, this is true. The devil, however, lies in the details, which are not spelled out in the document and will have to be negotiated.

President Poroshenko has made clear that he is willing to grant eastern Ukraine a degree of decentralization and local autonomy as long as that does not infringe upon the Kiev government's powers to decide and implement issues of national policy. However, Putin's plan goes well beyond anything envisaged by Poroshenko. Putin wants a radical restructuring of power that would turn the country into a federation of largely autonomous regions, with de facto veto power over membership in NATO and efforts to develop a closer political and economic association with the EU.

The October Parliamentary Elections

The hand of the pro-European forces has been strengthened by the results of the parliamentary elections held on October 26, 2014, which demonstrated strong support for the pro-European forces in Ukraine. Prime Minister Arseniy Yatsenyuk's People's Front came in first place, winning 22.2 percent of the popular vote, closely followed by Poroshenko's Bloc, which gained 21.8 percent of the popular vote. The

---

[10]   See Anthony Faiola, "Ukraine's President Offers Deal to the Separatists as Truce Frays," *Washington Post*, September 16, 2014.

new reformist party Self-Help, led by Andriy Sadoviy, mayor of Lviv, obtained 11 percent of the vote. Together, the three Pro-European parties have a solid majority in parliament, giving Ukraine the most pro-European parliament in its history.

Former prime minister Yulia Tymoshenko's party, the Fatherland Front, received 5.7 percent of the vote, just barely enough to cross the 5 percent threshold needed to secure representation in the Rada (parliament). The party is likely to support Yatsenyuk and Poroshenko's parties on most issues, strengthening the pro-European orientation in Ukrainian politics. The poor showing of the Fatherland Front suggests that the once popular and fiery Tymoshenko no longer commands much support among the Ukrainian electorate and is regarded as a figure of the past.

The Opposition Bloc, the remnant of Yanukovych's Party of Regions, received 9.7 percent of the vote. For the first time since Ukraine's independence in 1991, the Communist Party failed to obtain enough votes to be represented in the Rada.

The far right and nationalist parties Right Sector and Svoboda did poorly and failed to obtain sufficient votes to be represented in parliament as well. Right Sector obtained only 1.6 percent of the vote. This weak showing by the nationalist right makes it more difficult for the Russian media to credibly claim that Ukraine is led by a cabal of "Fascists" and "Neo-Nazis."

The Bumpy Road Ahead

The strong showing by the pro-European forces in the October parliamentary elections underscores the high degree of support in western and central Ukraine for closer ties to Europe and the EU. However, the Ukrainian government faces a difficult uphill battle to achieve internal and external stability. Several critical challenges stand out in the period ahead.

Pursuing Reform and Reducing Corruption

The first challenge is to implement a coherent and sustainable domestic reform agenda. Much will depend on the ability of Prime Minister Yatsenyuk and President Poroshenko to work together and avoid the internal bickering and divisive rivalries that plagued reform efforts during the Yushchenko-Tymoshenko period and contributed to the ultimate collapse of the Orange Revolution and Yanukovych's victory in the February 2010 presidential election.

The key question is whether the poisonous disunity and internal squabbles that contributed to the collapse of the Orange Revolution will reemerge and prevent Ukraine from pursuing a coherent reform program that will enable Kiev to forge closer ties to Europe. Poroshenko and Yatsenyuk worked well together and cooperated closely during the months following Putin's annexation of Crimea. But during the parliamentary electoral campaign, differences and signs of tension were visible. If they continue, they could be cause for concern.

Ukraine finds itself in a highly vulnerable situation today largely due to bad decisions by its own political leadership.[11] The previous leaders put off needed economic reforms because they feared the consequences for their own political power and interests. Many, particularly former president Yanukovych, put personal power and greed ahead of the national interest.

A related challenge is posed by the rampant and widespread corruption. Corruption reached alarming dimensions under Yanukovych. Prime Minister Yatsenyuk has accused Yanukovych of stealing $37 billion from the state—equal to one-fifth of Ukraine's gross domestic product (GDP) in 2013—during his four years in office.[12]

Meeting Energy Needs

Energy security represents another critical challenge. Ukraine depends on Russia for 60 percent of its natural gas. In the Soviet period, Russia

---

[11] See Steven Pifer, "Taking Stock in Ukraine," *The American Interest*, October 28, 2014.

[12] For a detailed discussion of the disruptive impact of corruption on Ukrainian economic and social life, see Anders Aslund, "Ukraine's Old Internal Enemy," *Wall Street Journal*, October 1, 2014.

kept the price artificially low, but in the past few years Ukraine has had to pay world market prices for Russian gas. In June 2014, Russia cut off gas supplies to Ukraine because of its failure to pay its back energy debts. The cutoff did not have much effect on Ukraine in the warm summer months, but with the onset of winter, Ukraine's energy problems may become more acute.

Ukraine has managed to stockpile 16 billion cubic meters of gas in underground storage tanks. It needs 5 billion cubic meters of gas beyond what it has stored to satisfy winter demands. The dispute with Russia over gas has already forced the Ukrainian government to ration domestically produced gas by cutting centrally provided hot water to flats, but more drastic measures may be necessary in the future unless the dispute with Russia over gas is quickly resolved.

A new gas agreement with Russia, brokered by the EU, was signed at the end of October 2014. Under the terms of the agreement, Ukraine will pay Gazprom, the Russian state-controlled energy giant, $5.3 billion toward its outstanding debt by the end of December 2014, using money it has borrowed from the International Monetary Fund. In addition, Kiev will make prepayments of $1.5 billion for 4 billion cubic meters of gas that Gazprom will provide for the remainder of the winter, again largely drawing on Western credits. This will enable Ukraine to obtain sufficient gas to make it through the winter.[13] However, while the gas deal with Russia resolves Ukraine's most immediate energy problem, the agreement represents only a temporary respite. The gas wars between Russia and Ukraine are unlikely to end until the two countries reach a political accommodation over eastern Ukraine.

Kiev also needs a viable energy policy. Ukraine is one of the most energy-inefficient countries in the world and needs to reduce its high level of energy wastage. It pays fuel subsidies equivalent to 7.5 percent of its GDP. Its energy intensity—the ration of energy used to economic output—is twice that of Russia and ten times the Organisation for Economic Co-operation and Development (OECD) average.[14] A

---

[13]   Christian Oliver, Jack Farchy, and Roman Olearchyk, "Moscow and Kiev Reach Deal on Gas Flows," *Financial Times*, October 31, 2014.

[14]   Oliver, Farchy, and Olearchyk, 2014.

reduction in subsidies and higher fuel bills are unavoidable if Ukraine is to solve its energy problems. The Ukrainian authorities introduced an increase in the price of gas of more than 50 percent for consumers and 40 percent for businesses. But further cuts in subsidies, while painful, will be needed if Ukraine is to achieve energy efficiency.

Managing Relations with Moscow

The final challenge relates to managing relations with Moscow, and this may be the most difficult challenge of all. The cease-fire agreed upon in Minsk on September 5, 2014, is fragile, and there is a serious danger that it will collapse. Putin has shown no sign of being willing to abide by the agreement. On the contrary, he has increased the military pressure on Ukraine. Russia has continued to covertly send tanks and other heavy equipment across the Russian-Ukrainian border in an attempt to bolster the pro-Russian separatists.[15] In addition, an estimated 200–300 regular Russian army troops are engaged in training and equipping the Ukrainian rebels in Ukraine.[16]

These military moves are a violation of the cease-fire agreement and suggest that the separatists, backed by Moscow, may be preparing to retake territory they lost to the Ukrainian army in early summer. One of their main objectives of the military activities is likely to be to support the separatist seizure of the port of Mariupol, which would enable Russia to supply the rebels by sea.

Putin's goal appears to be to turn eastern Ukraine into another long-term "frozen conflict," with the breakaway territories established in parts of Donetsk and Luhansk remaining outside of Kiev's control. These two oblasts would either be annexed and incorporated into Russia proper, like Crimea, or be independent entities closely linked economically and politically with Russia.

At the moment, Putin is riding high. His popular support and approval ratings have soared since the annexation of Crimea, reaching

---

[15]   Karoun Demirjian and Michael Birnbaum, "Ukraine Accuses Russia of an Incursion," *Washington Post*, November 8, 2014.

[16]   Michael R. Gordon and Andrew E. Kramer, "Russia Continues to Train and Equip Ukrainian Rebels, NATO Official Says," *New York Times*, November 4, 2014.

a record 85 percent in August. Meanwhile Europe is entering a period of recession and has little stomach for a confrontation with Russia. This may embolden Putin to test the United States' willingness and readiness to defend its interests.

One need only read Putin's speech to the Valdai Discussion Club on October 24, 2014, to get a sense of how difficult the coming period in U.S.-Russian relations is likely to be.[17] The speech was vintage Putin—angry, resentful, and self-righteous—blaming all ills on the West, especially the United States. It was reminiscent of his controversial speech at the Munich Security Conference in February 2007 in both tone and content.[18] Russia, Putin made clear, would be guided by its own national interests and stood adamantly opposed to Washington's efforts to build a unipolar world order. In the months ahead, Putin is likely to continue to chip away at Ukrainian sovereignty and test U.S. resolve, not only in Ukraine but elsewhere on Europe's periphery. The Baltic states in particular could face new pressures.

---

[17]   See Official Site of the President of Russia, "Meeting of the Valdai International Discussion Club," October 24, 2014. The Valdai Discussion Club is gathering of prominent Western politicians, academics, and journalists.

[18]   Vladimir Putin, prepared remarks before the 43rd Munich Conference on Security, Munich, Germany, February 12, 2007.

CHAPTER THREE

Implications for the United States

Under Putin, Russia has become a revisionist state. Putin believes that the European security order that emerged at the end of the Cold War does not reflect Russia's interests. He wants to refashion it in ways that are more compatible with Russian interests and restore what he sees as Russia's rightful place in Europe. He regards the post-Soviet space as a sphere of Russia's "privileged interest" and seeks to block the penetration of this space by Western values and institutions—not only NATO but also the European Union.

What is emerging is a "Cool War." This "Cool War" is quite different from the Cold War of the 1950s through the 1980s.[1] It is regionally rather than globally focused and primarily aimed at maintaining, and where possible increasing, Russian influence in Europe, especially the post-Soviet space. However, while the "Cool War" is more limited than the Cold War, it could lead to a broad deterioration of political, economic, and military relations between Russia and the Atlantic Alliance and spill over into other important areas, such as arms control. For example, Russia might decide to leave the Intermediate-Range Nuclear Forces (INF) Treaty to facilitate the deployment of a new generation of

---

[1] The term "Cool War" seems appropriate since it acknowledges that the nature of the enhanced competition between Russia and the Atlantic Alliance will be much more complex and dynamic given the extensive economic and financial relations between both parties. This complex relationship of defense, deterrence, competition, and cooperation is not unlike the emerging geostrategic relations between the United States and China. For a discussion of the concept of an Asian "Cool War," see Paul K. Davis and Peter A. Wilson, *Looming Discontinuities in U.S. Military Strategy and Defense Planning—Colliding RMAs Necessitate a New Strategy*, Santa Monica, Calif.: RAND Corporation, OP-326, 2011.

ground mobile long-range precision-guided land attack cruise missiles (LACMs). Such a move would cast a long shadow on the prospects of any future nuclear arms control and disarmament agreements between Washington and Moscow. Under a very bad case scenario, even the fate of the New START agreement could be put at risk.

U.S. and European Interests

In the face of this evolving challenge, maintaining close coordination of U.S. and European policy will be critically important—but also more difficult. There is an asymmetry of interest between the United States and Europe when it comes to Russia. Europe is more dependent on Russian energy than the United States. Europe also conducts a larger portion of its foreign trade with Russia. Hence the United States' European allies, especially Germany and Italy, are more hesitant to impose sanctions on Russia. As a result, adopting a common policy with which both sides are comfortable has been difficult.

Initially the EU, especially Germany and Italy, was hesitant to impose a third round of sanctions on Russia. It was only after the Malaysian commercial airliner was shot down that the EU agreed to impose sanctions on Russia's energy, defense, and financial sectors. Indeed, had the Malaysian airliner not been shot down, the EU probably would not have agreed to impose such biting sanctions.

Russia responded to the imposition of the sanctions on its energy, defense, and financial sectors by announcing a ban on fruits and vegetables from the EU, the United States, Australia, Canada, and Norway. Russian officials, including Prime Minister Dmitry Medvedev, made clear that other "protective measures" were under consideration on industrial sectors such as car-making and aircraft production.

The use of bans on agricultural products is hardly new. Russia has placed restrictions on Georgian and Moldovan produce as well as the import of Polish apples. But the restrictions imposed in retaliation for the sanctions by the United States and EU are on a much broader scale. Russia is the largest foreign market for sales of fruit and vegetables from the EU and the second-biggest for American poultry. While in the medium to long run the losses can be offset by import substitution, in the short run they could spark price increases and shortage for Russian consumers.

The ban is likely to have little impact on the United States because, with exception of poultry, the United States exports relatively few agricultural products or food goods to Russia— about $1.3 billion in 2013. This represented about 11 percent of the exports to Russia but less than 1 percent of all American agriculture exports, or less than 0.1 percent of total exports.[2]

The situation is quite different for Europe. Russia is a fast-growing market for European farmers. The East European EU members, especially Poland and Lithuania, will be the biggest losers from the ban. Germany and Netherlands will be affected along with Spain and Italy, but not as much as the East European countries.

The group hardest hit by the ban, however, is likely to be the Russian consumer, especially the middle class.[3] Putin appears to be gambling that the Russian population will blame the West, not him, for any shortages and price increases that are triggered by the ban on fruits and vegetables. At the same time, he may be signaling that at a time of increasing geopolitical competition with the West, Russia needs to reduce its importation of foreign food and return to a more autarkic policy, similar to the one pursued by the Soviet Union during the Cold War.

The Economic Dimension

Security and geopolitical considerations have been the key drivers behind Putin's policy. He appears to have paid scant attention to the economic impact of his actions. Putin seems to have believed that the Europeans, particularly Germany, would not agree to impose serious

---

[2]   "Putin schockt die Bauern in Osteuropa," *Frankfurter Allgemeine Zeitung*, August 8, 2014

[3]   "Importverbot trifft russische Mittelschicht," *Frankfurter Allgemeine Zeitung*, August 11, 2014.

sanctions against Russia in retaliation for his intervention in eastern Ukraine. This belief is likely to prove to be one of his most important miscalculations.

The Russian economy had already begun to show signs of a slow-down in growth and investment before the Crimean crisis. However, the sharp decline in the price of oil, the impact of Western sanctions, and the increasing threat of recession have caused growing concern in Russian business circles. As of December 2014, the ruble had lost half its value since the beginning of the year. This decline poses a danger of stimulating a currency crisis on the scale of 1998 or 2008.

But there is an important difference between those crises and the situation now. Today's loss of confidence in the ruble is due not just to economic or financial factors, but also to geopolitical factors. The ruble's decline reflects fears that the cease-fire signed in Minsk on September 5, 2014, is unraveling and that the separatists, backed by Russia, may be planning a new offensive. This sense of growing risk and uncertainty has driven the value of ruble much lower than would be expected from a 20 percent decline in oil prices

Many Russian businessmen have begun to send their money abroad. Capital flight was expected to hit a record $120 billion in 2014, perhaps even slightly higher.[4] Inflation, aggravated by the ban on many Western food imports, is rising. At the same time, declining oil prices and signs of a deepening recession threaten to undercut Putin's defense spending drive.

The draft budget for 2015–2017 calls for a cut in defense expenditures by 5.3 percent in 2016, the first cut in defense spending since 2008.[5] The drop in the price of oil to below $50 per barrel has caused unease in the Russian business community. Government officials have warned that the budget can be balanced over the next three years only if oil prices remain above $100 per barrel.[6]

---

[4]   "Putin Is Leading Russia Down an Isolationist Path," *Financial Times*, October 8, 2014

[5]   Kathrin Hille, "Russia to Curb Defense Spending," *Financial Times*, October 13, 2014.

[6]   David M. Herszenhorn, "Fall in Oil Prices Poses a Problem for Russia, Iraq and Others," *New York Times*, October 16, 2014.

Putin does not appear to share these concerns. In the short term, Russia does not face a serious threat as a result of the sharp decline in oil prices. It has over $430 billion in foreign currency reserves that can be used to cushion the effect of the drop in the price of oil if it remains below $100 a barrel for an extended period of time. However, in the longer run, persistently low oil prices, reinforced by the pressure imposed by Western sanctions, could pose a serious challenge to the Putin regime.[7]

Putin's popularity rests on two central pillars: his appeal to Russian nationalism and a rise in the economic standard of living. If the standard of living begins to drop, Putin's popularity could erode, and he could face growing social discontent, particularly among the middle class in the major cities. This could have two possible effects. The first is that Putin tries to defuse rising discontent by seeking an accommodation with the West. The second—and more probable—alternative is that he seeks to deflect attention away from Russia's growing economic woes by stoking the fires of Russian nationalism and intensifying military pressure on Ukraine and/or staging a provocation in one of the Baltic states.

Russia's Pivot Toward China

The United States is not the only country that has begun to focus more attention on Asia. As relations with the West have soured and become more difficult, Putin has sought to expand relations with China, especially in the energy field. While the opening to China began prior to the eruption of the Ukrainian crisis, the sanctions imposed by the United States and EU have given the opening to Beijing greater impetus.

In May 2014, Russia and China signed a $400 billion deal to provide natural gas to China over 30 years. The details of the May gas deal have not been published, but Russian media accounts suggest that China got a favorable deal because Putin needed to show that Russia could survive even if trade relations with Europe declined.

---

[7]   See Sergei Guriev, "Russia Can't Withstand Lower Oil Prices Forever," *Financial Times*, October 20, 2014.

The May agreement was followed by the signing of 38 major agreements by Chinese Premier Li Keqiang and Russian Prime Minister Medvedev in October, including a currency swap and tax treaty. The two sides also hope to sign another major energy deal in the near future involving the construction of a natural gas pipeline to western China.

The agreements signed in 2014 are the centerpiece of Putin's Eastern policy. When the first of these, the "Power of Siberia" pipeline to eastern China, reaches capacity, it will ship a volume equal to nearly one-quarter of Russia's 2013 gas exports to Europe. If the second pipeline (the "Altay" route to western China) is built, the total could eventually exceed 40 percent.[8]

However, as Thane Gustafson has noted, heading east is not the same as getting there.[9] There are a number of serious obstacles to orienting Russia's gas industry toward China. Russia's entire gas industry has been concentrated in the western third of the country. Shifting the industry's center of gravity eastward is an enormous undertaking and requires developing a whole new industry from scratch. This cannot be done overnight. Even on the most ambitious time table, the "Power of Siberia" line will not reach its full capacity of 38 billion cubic meters per year until the mid-2030s.

The pipeline is also enormously expensive—it could cost as much as $55 billion for the eastern route alone.[10] The Western sanctions have further complicated Russia's attempted pivot. Although Gazprom is not directly subject to U.S. and European sanctions, the measures taken by Washington and Brussels have severely circumscribed the ability of Russian firms to borrow money. To finance the Power of Siberia pipeline, Gazprom will have to raise money on the international markets, where prospects are uncertain.

These problems notwithstanding, Putin's pivot toward China represents an important shift in Russian policy, and its significance should

---

[8]   Thane Gustafson, "Russia May Pivot to the East But It Cannot Escape Its European Destiny," *Financial Times*, November 20, 2014.

[9]   Gustafson, 2014.

[10]   Gustafson, 2014.

not be underestimated. In the energy field, Russia and China are natural partners. Russia has bountiful supplies of gas and oil, while China's energy needs are rapidly expanding, creating a growing necessity to find new resources. These expanding energy ties are bound to have an impact on political ties, creating new interdependencies.

At the same time, one should not exaggerate the nature of the expanding ties between Moscow and Beijing. At its core, the closer ties represent a marriage of convenience rather than a blooming love affair between two like-minded partners. Russia and China both share an interest in constraining U.S. advances in Asia, but there are objective limits to the partnership. Russia is a declining power and junior partner in the relationship. Given its large investments in the U.S. economy, Beijing will want to keep the door open to cooperation with the United States and not burn its bridges with Washington.

Constraints on U.S.-European Cooperation

Economic factors may also have an impact on European policy, driving European leaders to adopt a cautious approach toward Russia. There are signs that the crisis in Ukraine and growing tensions with Russia may be pushing the Eurozone back into recession.[11] During the first quarter of 2014, the economies of seven out of 18 Eurozone countries shrank, while France had zero growth. Italy's gross GDP contracted 0.2 percent from April through June 2014. The decline dashed hopes that Italy, the third-largest economy in the Eurozone behind Germany and France, was finally emerging from a decade of stagnation.[12]

In addition, there are indications that the German economy, which provides more than one-quarter of the Eurozone's output, is losing momentum.[13] Germany's industrial output fell 4 percent between July and August 2014—the biggest monthly decline since 2009. The sluggish industrial figures show that Germany has begun to suffer from a

---

[11] Jack Ewing and Gala Pianigiana, "Slowdown in Italy Adds to Fears Over Ukraine," *International New York Times*, August 7, 2014.

[12] Ewing and Pianigiana, 2014.

[13] Claire Jones, "Russian Tensions Hit Fragile Eurozone Growth," *Financial Times*, August 11, 2014.

weakening of demand for its exports, raising fears that Germany might be headed for a recession. Earlier expectations that Germany could lift the weaker economies in the Eurozone out of the doldrums now look highly doubtful. Instead, it looks increasingly likely that the Eurozone will slide into its third recession since the financial crisis in 2008.[14]

The escalating sanction regimes imposed by the United States and Europe have sent jitters through European financial circles. Leading figures in the European financial world, such as Mario Draghi, President of the European Central Bank, fear that a further breakdown of relations with Russia over Ukraine could weaken European growth in the second half of 2014. This may make European political leaders more reluctant in the future to impose additional sanctions on Russia and could generate increasing pressure to roll back some of the restrictions already in place.

EU-Russian Relations

The Ukrainian crisis has put the EU and Russia on an increasing collision course—a course that neither side wanted nor foresaw. As Ulrich Speck has noted, the EU never intended to get into a geopolitical confrontation with Russia; rather, it "sleepwalked" into it.[15] But now the geopolitical stakes are too high for either side to easily back down.

For the EU, two important interests are at stake: first, the stabilization of a zone of instability and turmoil on its Eastern periphery, and second, respect for the principle that European borders cannot be changed by force. This has been a core principle of EU policy since the signing of the Helsinki Final Act in 1975, and it was violated by Russia's annexation of Crimea. Thus, the EU's credibility as a united and important international actor is on the line.

---

[14]   Chris Giles and Stefan Wagstyl, "IMF Warns of Third Eurozone Recession Since Financial Crisis," *Financial Times*, October 8, 2014.

[15]   Ulrich Speck, "How the EU Sleepwalked into a Conflict with Russia," *Carnegie Europe*, July 10, 2014.

The stakes for Russia are also high. A pro-European Ukraine would be seen as a strategic defeat and humiliation for both Russia and Putin personally. Without Ukraine, Putin's plan for a Eurasian Union makes little sense and is unlikely to be realized.

Initially, Russia did not see the EU as a threat. Most of its attention was devoted to trying to block the enlargement of NATO. However, Russian attitudes began to change with the development in 2009 of the EU's Eastern Partnership. A joint Polish-Swedish initiative, the Eastern Partnership was designed to increase cooperation with six states in the post-Soviet space: Ukraine, Belarus, Moldova, Armenia, Azerbaijan, and Georgia. However, the Eastern Partnership never had the full support of the strongest EU member states, particularly Germany, which feared that the initiative could have a negative impact on its attempt to deepen relations with Russia.

Those in the EU who supported the Eastern Partnership saw it as a win-win situation for all concerned. EU officials believed the initiative could forge closer ties to Russia's neighbors in the post-Soviet space and simultaneously maintain good relations with Moscow. Russia, they argued, would benefit from greater stabilization of its periphery, and the members of the Eastern Partnership could act as a bridge between Russia and the EU.

Moscow, however, never shared this view. To Russian officials, the Eastern Partnership looked more like a "hostile takeover." Rather, Russia intended the six states targeted by the Eastern Partnership to be part of the Eurasian Customs Union—later renamed the Eurasian Union—and confronted members with a stark either/or choice: Membership in the Eurasian Union was incompatible with the deep and comprehensive trade agreements that the EU sought to sign with the members of the Eastern Partnership.

Ukraine tried to have it both ways—to expand ties to the EU and simultaneously maintain good relations with Moscow. For a time, this strategy looked as if it might work. However, on the eve of the opening of the EU summit in Vilnius in November 2013, Yanukovych, under heavy pressure from Putin, refused to sign the Association Agreement, and it was withdrawn from the summit agenda. Yanukovych's refusal to sign the Association Agreement sparked widespread protests calling for the agreement to be signed and a strengthening of cooperation with the EU, which culminated in Yanukovych's ouster as president in February 2014 and the signing of the of the Association Agreement in July 2014.

However, Putin has not given up and is attempting to block implementation of the Association Agreement. In a letter to Josef Manuel Barroso, President of the European Commission, in late September, he demanded the reopening of the negotiations on the agreement and threatened to take "immediate and appropriate retaliatory measures" if Ukraine seeks to implement the agreement.[16]

The German Factor

The Ukrainian crisis has underscored Germany's increasingly important geopolitical role in managing relations with Russia. Berlin is Russia's most important trading partner in Europe, and a key market for energy. Ties between Berlin and Moscow were particularly close under Merkel's predecessor Gerhard Schroeder (SPD), especially in the economic field. (On leaving office, Schroeder became a well-paid executive for Gazprom, the Russian state energy giant.) While Merkel has been more outspoken about criticizing Russian abuses of human and political rights, her economic policy toward Russia has until very recently differed little from Schroeder's.

However, German policy has begun to shift lately. Merkel was the driving force behind the tough sanctions adopted by the EU in July. Initially, Merkel had hoped that she could nudge Putin toward a diplomatic solution. But after the shooting down of the Malaysian airliner, Merkel lost trust in Putin, because she believed he had repeatedly lied to her about Russia's involvement and his willingness to restrain the separatists.[17] As the months have passed, her tone has sharpened and

---

[16]   Peter Spiegel, "Putin Demands Reopening of EU Trade Pact with Ukraine," *Financial Times*, September 26, 2014.

[17]   See Quentin Peel, "Merkel Wants a Stable World and Is Willing to Pay a Price," *Financial Times*, August 12, 2014. See also Stefan Wagstyl, "Merkel Rethink on Tough Action Reflects Loss of Trust in Putin," *Financial Times*, July 31, 2014.

she has become more outspoken in her criticism of Russian policy and Putin personally.

From Berlin's perspective, Russia has gone in one year from being a difficult partner to being an adversary. The attempt to intensify cooperation in a number of areas launched in 2008—one in which German leaders placed great hopes—appears to have come to an irrevocable end.[18] Instead, Berlin is currently discussing ways in which it can blunt Moscow's expansionary drive, particularly in the Balkans.

The tougher policy toward Russia has been given important impetus by the Ukrainian crisis and reflects Germany's willingness to take on greater international responsibility and leadership—a willingness first officially broached by President Joachim Gauck at the Munich Security Conference in February 2014, where he called for Germany to do more "to guarantee the security that others have provided it for decades."[19] Foreign Minister Frank-Walter Steinmeier (a Social Democrat) and Defense Minister Ursula von der Leyen, a member of Merkel's Christian Democratic Party (CDU), raised similar themes in their remarks at the conference.[20]

This new willingness to take on more international responsibility represents an important shift in German policy. In the past, Germany has been the dominant European player on economic issues—as its tough-minded defense of the need for austerity measures and greater belt-tightening during the Eurozone crisis underscored. However, until very recently Berlin has been reluctant to take the lead on foreign policy issues, which have traditionally been left to France and Britain. However, the Eurozone crisis underscored the need for a bolder, more assertive German role.

Merkel was initially reluctant to assume that role for fear of sparking historical concerns about German "dominance." However,

---

[18] "Putin's Reach: Merkel Concerned About Russian Influence in the Balkans," *Der Spiegel*, November 17, 2014.

[19] See Joachim Gauck, "Germany's Role in the World: Reflections on Responsibility, Norms and Alliances," speech at the Opening of the Munich Security Conference, January 31, 2014.

[20] See Frank-Walter Steinmeier, Foreign Minister, speech at the 50th Munich Security Conference, January 31, 2014; and Ursula von der Leyen, speech at the 50th Munich Security Conference, January 31, 2014.

faced with a leadership vacuum, Merkel had little choice and reluctantly stepped forward to fill it. As noted, she played a critical role in shaping the tougher EU sanctions adopted in July 2014. This was all the more striking because in the past Germany has often refrained from taking actions that could antagonize Russia and has often shown "understanding" for some of Moscow's policies—a tendency which has angered many East European members of NATO and the EU.

The United States needs to build on the close cooperation with Berlin that emerged during the sanctions debate to forge closer ties to Germany. Close coordination of German and U.S. policy will be more important than ever in the future because of Germany's increasing economic clout and its special relationship with Russia.

Washington should welcome and encourage Germany's willingness to take on greater international responsibility, which is very much in U.S. interests. At the same time, Washington needs to be sensitive to the domestic constraints that make this effort to change the German "culture of reticence" a difficult task; a large part of the German population is uncomfortable with Germany playing a more active international role.[21] Thus, Washington should recognize that it will take time for the German public to adapt to such a role.

Finally, there is a critical need to rebuild mutual trust in the wake of the NSA spying revelations and other intelligence incidents. It is hard to overdramatize the damage that these revelations have done to U.S. interests and image among the German public. The United States needs to make a conscious and sustained effort to begin to rebuild trust among the German population.

The NATO Factor

Ukraine's ties to NATO have been a source of serious tension in Kiev's relations with Moscow. Russia is viscerally opposed to Ukrainian mem-

---

[21] According to a recent poll, only 30 percent of the German population favors Germany taking on greater responsibility in international affairs, while 70 percent are opposed, some quite strongly. See Majid Sattar, "Schlussetappe auf dem langen Weg nach Westen," *Frankfurter Allgemeine Zeitung*, August 26, 2014.

bership in NATO and has fought hard to block Ukrainian membership in the Alliance. Ukraine's entry into NATO would alter the balance of power in Central Europe to Russia's disadvantage and foreclose any residual possibility of building a "Slavic Union" composed of Russia, Ukraine, and Belarus. Thus, Russia has made preventing Ukrainian membership in NATO one of its top foreign policy priorities.

Ukraine's policy toward NATO has evolved considerably in the past decade. In the early years after independence, Ukraine pursued a nonaligned policy, in part to avoid antagonizing Russia. Kiev initially opposed NATO enlargement to Central Europe because it feared that NATO membership would create new dividing lines in Europe and lead to increased Russian pressure on Ukraine. However, Moscow's hardline opposition to NATO enlargement and Kiev's desire to improve relations with the West contributed to a gradual shift in Ukraine's approach to enlargement.

Under President Leonid Kuchma, Ukraine consciously began to strengthen ties to the Alliance. Ukraine was the first member of the Commonwealth of Independent States to join Partnership for Peace (PfP) and has been one of the most active participants in PfP exercises. At the NATO summit in Madrid in July 1997, Kiev signed the Charter on a Distinctive Partnership with NATO. Although the charter did not provide explicit security guarantees, it called for the establishment of a crisis consultative mechanism that could be activated if Ukraine perceived a direct threat to its security.[22]

The charter also foresaw a broad expansion of ties between NATO and Ukraine in a number of key areas, such as civil-military relations, democratic control of the armed forces, armaments cooperation, and defense planning. In addition to a close relationship with NATO, Ukraine also built individual security relationships with Britain and the United States.

---

[22] For the text of the charter, see "Charter on A Distinctive Partnership Between the North Atlantic Treaty Organization and Ukraine," *NATO Review*, Vol. 45, No. 4, July–August 1997, Documentation Section. See also David Buchan and David White, "NATO Signs Charter with Ukraine," *Financial Times*, July 10, 1997.

The rapprochement with NATO was not undertaken because Ukraine felt a strong military threat. Rather it was part of a carefully calculated political balancing act pursued by President Kuchma, who sought to strengthen ties to NATO as a means of increasing his political leverage with Moscow. Contrary to the concerns of many critics who feared that intensifying ties to NATO would lead to a sharp deterioration of relations with Russia, the rapprochement with NATO increased Ukraine's freedom of maneuver and led to an improvement of ties with Moscow.

In May 2002, President Kuchma announced that Ukraine intended to abandon its policy of nonalignment and apply for NATO membership. Here again the decision was part of a calculated effort to counterbalance Russia. President Putin's decision to support the United States in the war on terrorism and the subsequent improvement in U.S.-Russian relations raised the prospect that Russia would have a closer relationship with NATO than Ukraine. Ukraine's application for NATO membership was designed to undercut this prospect.

However, Kuchma's increasingly repressive internal policies as well as suspicions that Ukraine had sold aircraft tracking systems to Iraq (the Kolchuga affair) led NATO to put relations with Ukraine on hold. The Alliance decided to wait until after the 2004 presidential elections before taking any new initiatives with Ukraine.

The election of Viktor Yushchenko as Ukrainian president in December 2004 resulted in a warming of Ukraine's relations with NATO. In an attempt to encourage Yushchenko's pro-Western reform course, NATO offered Ukraine Intensified Dialogue status in April 2005—a preparatory step toward an individualized Membership Action Plan (MAP). In the run up to the NATO summit in Bucharest in April 2008, President Bush pushed hard for the Alliance to grant Ukraine and Georgia MAP status. MAP was viewed by many, especially the Russian leadership, as being a precursor to NATO membership. France and Germany, however, opposed granting Ukraine MAP, fearing that it would antagonize Russia and lead to a deterioration of the Alliance's relations with Russia. France and Germany succeeded in blocking efforts to grant MAP to Ukraine and Georgia. However, the communiqué issued at the end of the summit by the NATO Heads of

State and Governments stated that Ukraine and Georgia would one day be admitted to NATO, although no specific date or timetable was mentioned. Thus, from Moscow's point of view, the outcome was even worse than the Russian leadership had expected. It appeared that while Ukraine and Georgia had been denied MAP, they had been given a formal commitment that they would one day become members of NATO, with all the implications articulated above.

However, since the conclusion of the Bucharest summit, the prospects for Ukraine's entry into NATO have significantly declined. The Russian invasion of Georgia contributed to a shift in thinking within the Alliance about NATO's enlargement to the post-Soviet space, and especially Ukrainian membership. The invasion was a sharp reminder that membership in NATO is not a one-way street; it also involves concrete commitments and responsibilities, including a commitment to use force if a NATO member is attacked. At the same time, the invasion made clear Russia's readiness to defend its interests—with force if necessary. Hence, in the aftermath of the Russian invasion of Georgia, the issue of NATO membership for Ukraine and Georgia was put on indefinite hold. While the door to Ukrainian and Georgian membership in NATO remained open rhetorically, in practice membership for both countries was shelved and relegated to the back burner.

In the aftermath of Russia's annexation of Crimea and attempt to destabilize eastern Ukraine, the issue of Ukrainian membership in NATO has again come to the fore. Some U.S. officials and analysts suggest that the United States should respond to the annexation of Crimea and the attempt to destabilize eastern Ukraine by admitting Ukraine into NATO. However, such a move would be unwise. Given Russia's strong opposition to Ukrainian membership in NATO, actively pushing for Ukrainian membership at this point would be counterproductive and could be highly destabilizing. It would only inflame the political atmosphere and could give Putin an excuse for taking military action against Kiev.

Instead the emphasis in NATO policy will likely be on modernizing Ukraine's military and security forces and improving their readiness and training. Should this happen, the Army would have an important role to play in this program. However, given the years of neglect of the military and the rampant corruption in Ukrainian armed forces, U.S. officials should have no illusions about the difficulties such an effort would face. There are no quick fixes to the problems confronting the Ukrainian armed forces. The problems are structural and cannot be repaired overnight. Fixing them will require a long-term, sustained commitment to structural reform on the part of the United States and NATO.

Reassuring Eastern Europe

The Russian annexation of Crimea and attempt to destabilize eastern Ukraine have made Poland and the Baltic countries very nervous and prompted calls for NATO to station combat forces in Eastern Europe and the Baltic states. The main outcome of NATO's summit in Wales in September was an emphasis on deterrence and reassurance of NATO's new Central and East European members. At Wales, NATO approved plans for the creation of a Very High Readiness Joint Task Force (VJTF), a brigade-sized (4,000-man) rapid reaction force within the NATO Response Force (NRF) that could be dispatched to East European trouble spots within several days.[23] This upgraded force is designed to enhance NATO's ability to effectively carry out crisis management missions in regions far from NATO members' capitals. The NATO Standing Naval Forces will also be given greater emphasis. In addition, the Alliance agreed to continue air policing over the Baltic states and to beef up its multinational headquarters in Poland.

---

[23] Stephen Erlanger, Julie Herschfeld Davis, and Stephen Castle, "NATO Plans a Special Force to Reassure Eastern Europe and Deter Russia," *New York Times*, September 6, 2014. For a detailed discussion, see Jeffrey A. Larson, "The Wales Summit and NATO's Deterrence Capabilities: An Assessment," NDC Research Report, NATO Defense College, November 2014.

Strengthening Baltic Security

The sense of vulnerability is particularly strong in the Baltic states. Baltic officials note that under Putin the number of incidents and violations of Baltic airspace have significantly increased. NATO fighter planes policing Baltic airspace were scrambled 68 times along Lithuania's borders—the highest count by far in more than ten years. Latvia registered 150 "close incidents." Finland has had five violations of its airspace against a yearly average of one or two in the previous decade.[24]

Some of this activity can be attributed to an increase in Russian military exercises along NATO's eastern borders. While the Baltic states have borne the brunt of the incursions, these violations and incidents have been part of a broader surge in infringements.

The incidents have not been limited to airspace incursions. According to Estonian officials, in early September a well-armed squad of Russian security operatives reportedly kidnapped an officer in the Estonian Internal Security Service, dragged him at gunpoint into Russia, and charged him with espionage before a squad of Russian television cameras.[25] Baltic officials see the incident as a blunt warning to the Balts that, despite their membership in NATO, Russia still has the capacity to act as it pleases in the Baltic region.

This is not to suggest that Russia is planning a conventional attack on the Baltic states. Such a scenario is highly unlikely. As members of NATO, the Baltic states have a security guarantee under Article V of the Washington treaty. Thus, a direct Russian conventional attack against any one of the Baltic states is unlikely. However, there are myriad ways in which Russia could put pressure on the Baltic states short of a conventional attack.

The fact that Estonia and Latvia have large ethnic Russian minorities on their territory provides a ready-made pretext for exerting pressure on the two Baltic states, especially since Putin has stressed Russia's

[24]   Richard Milne, Sam Jones, and Kathrin Hille, "Russian Air Incursions Rattle Baltic States," *Financial Times*, September 25, 2014.

[25]   Andrew Higgins, "Tensions Surge in Estonia Amid a Russian Replay of the Cold War," *New York Times*, October 6, 2014.

responsibility to protect the welfare of ethnic Russians and Russian speakers living outside Russia's borders. It is not hard to imagine a scenario in which Russia seeks to use the alleged "mistreatment" of the Russian minority in Estonia or Latvia as a pretext for making political demands on the two countries. This fact, combined with the difficulty of defending the Baltic states against Russia's overwhelming local military superiority, has generated concerns among Baltic officials that at some point Russia might try to use such claims as a pretext for putting pressure on one or more of the Baltic states.

As in Crimea and eastern Ukraine, Russia would not likely undertake an overt military invasion, but rather could attempt to utilize a combination of deception, clandestine sabotage, and strategic ambiguity to try to destabilize one or more of the Baltic states—measures designed to confuse and obfuscate efforts to attempt a creeping takeover of part of the Baltics.

If true, then this implies that in the future more attention needs to be paid to countering unconventional threats. Russian efforts to use unconventional approaches raise important questions that need to be answered by NATO and national planners: When does Article V apply? What is the threshold and how can it be identified before that threshold is crossed? What can and should be done, and by whom?[26]

President Obama's visit to Estonia on his way to the NATO summit in Wales in early September was important for strengthening the resolve of the Baltic allies. The stopover was designed to reassure the Baltic states that the United States and NATO were committed to their security. During his visit, Obama stressed that "the security of Tallinn, Riga and Vilnius is just as important as the defense of Berlin, Paris or London."[27] Should more concrete measures to enhance deterrence in the Baltic region be desired, options could include the following:

---

[26] We would like to express our gratitude to Robert Nurick for enhancing our awareness and understanding of the dilemmas posed by Russian use of nonlinear and hybrid warfare.

[27] See Julie Herschfeld Davis, "Obama in Estonia, Calls Ukraine Conflict 'A Moment of Truth,'" *New York Times*, September 3, 2014.

- **Increase the capacity of the Baltic interior defense forces,** including Special Weapons And Tactics (SWAT) teams, riot police, and motorized national police and intelligence services. Due to the possibility of Moscow inflaming the ethnic Russian community in the Baltic region, those countries may need to increase their internal intelligence and security forces.
- **Develop more robust homeland defense.** Although the military budgets of the Baltic nations are very limited, it is possible that certain key military capabilities could be enhanced. Examples include man-portable air defense missiles and infantry-portable anti-armor guided missiles that could be used to delay and inflict casualties on a Russian attack while NATO prepares a larger response.
- **Deploy a Baltic trip-wire force.** For this option, there are two variants:
  - Station NATO forces in the Baltic states. A NATO ground presence in the three Baltic states would greatly reinforce the Alliance's deterrent posture. This need not be a heavy force capable of defending territory, but rather could be simply a force large enough to make clear that, if it attacked, Russia would be choosing conflict with NATO. However, there is no consensus within the Alliance for taking such a bold step. While the new members, especially Poland, strongly favor permanently stationing NATO troops in Eastern Europe, Germany is adamantly opposed to such a move, fearing that it will further antagonize Moscow.
  - Depend upon rapid reaction forces. Similar to the emerging NATO Rapid Reaction concept, this option would rely on light air transportable forces that could be quickly deployed from locations in Europe or the United States. By design, these forces would not have the combat power of heavier armored motorized and mechanized/armored forces; however, they would provide a trip-wire force that also would erase any doubt that Russia was choosing armed conflict with NATO.
- **Deploy more than a trip-wire force to the Baltics.** The Atlantic Alliance might conclude that a very robust defense and deter-

rent posture is needed in the Baltic states to convince Russia of NATO's seriousness of purpose. A robust ground presence would dramatically raise the military stakes for Moscow, which could not defeat a determined NATO defense unless it went nuclear, but the political objections within NATO European countries will likely be similar to any decision to permanently deploy forces in the Baltic region.

- **Enhance rapid reaction capabilities and prepositioning.** NATO could enhance its air- and sea-transportable rapid reaction forces to provide it with more response options. Additionally, NATO could preposition of heavy equipment in Poland, Romania, and Germany. Given the geographic advantages Russia enjoys in the Baltic region, NATO leaders should be prepared to deploy these forces during a timely Flexible Deterrent Operation (FDO) in a strategically ambiguous environment; ensuring that the NATO contingents are able to respond rapidly to any aggressive Russian move, even if ambiguous, would be important.

Defense Cooperation with Sweden and Finland

Russian actions in Ukraine have intensified Sweden and Finland's interest in closer cooperation with NATO and given the debate regarding possible Swedish and Finnish membership in NATO new impetus. Although neither country is likely to join NATO in the next few years, both have stepped up defense cooperation with the Alliance recently. Finland and Sweden both signed host-nation support agreements with NATO at the Wales summit, indicating the readiness to receive assistance from Allied forces and to support them with their military assets, such as ships and aircraft.

As Andrew Michta has noted, Sweden and Finland are increasingly important to NATO's defense planning.[28] They offer a critical link for operations involving the Baltic states. Any decisions taken by

---

[28] See Andrew Michta, "Putin Targets the Scandinavians," *The American Interest*, November 17, 2014.

Sweden and Finland on possible NATO membership would have a ripple effect on the overall security position of the Baltic states and on Central European security in general.

Recently, Moscow has stepped up efforts to undo the budding cooperation between Sweden, Finland, and NATO and ultimately to neutralize the two countries through direct and indirect military, economic, and political means. Moscow's goal is to force the two Nordic states to opt out of any confrontation with Russia and prevent NATO from using their airspace and territory. Russian planning, exercises, and patterns of harassment seek to convey to Sweden and Finland that if Russia should choose to, it could target their territory as well. The goal is to undermine the confidence of Alliance members along the northeastern flank that NATO would carry out its Article V security guarantee.[29]

By targeting Sweden and Finland Russia seeks to achieve two important goals: (1) dissuade Sweden and Finland from joining NATO and (2) persuade the Baltic states that they can not rely on NATO's Article V security guarantee. If Moscow's effort is successful, it would not only decrease security in the Nordic-Baltic region but weaken NATO's credibility more broadly, quite possibly irreparably. Thus, there is an important linkage between Nordic-Baltic security and the broader security challenge posed by Russia's actions in Ukraine. U.S. and European leaders ignore this linkage at their peril.

New Uncertainties in the Black Sea Region

The annexation of Crimea has shifted the military balance in the Black Sea region more strongly in Russia's favor and significantly increased Russia's strategic footprint in the region. In addition to acquiring Sevastopol, the finest natural harbor in the Black Sea, Russia also acquired the former Crimean Ukrainian naval bases of Novoozerne on Donuzlav

---

[29] Michta, 2014.

Bay, Myrnyi (Donuzlav Lake), Saky, Balaklava, and a maritime infantry base at Feodosia.[30]

The expansion of the Black Sea Fleet will strengthen Russia's ability to project power in the region and enable Moscow to exert influence over the eastern Mediterranean, Balkans, and Middle East. Within the Black Sea littoral, the Bulgarian, Romanian, and Georgian navies are no match for the Black Sea Fleet.[31] Only Turkey is in a position to contest the maritime superiority of the Russian fleet. Turkey and Russia have been historical rivals for power in the Black Sea region. They have fought 13 wars with each other, most of which Turkey lost. This historical animosity was reinforced by Stalin's expansionist policy toward Turkey at the end of World War II, which was the driving force behind Turkey's decision to join NATO in 1952.

In the past decade, however, Turkey's relations with Russia have improved markedly, especially in the economic realm. Russia is Turkey's largest trading partner and its largest supplier of natural gas. Russia is also an important market for the Turkish construction industry. Projects in Russia account for about one-fourth of all projects carried out by Turkish contractors around the world.[32]

Energy has been an important driver of the recent intensification of ties between Ankara and Moscow. Russia supplies over 50 percent of Turkey's natural-gas imports and 40 percent of its crude oil imports. Russian investment in Turkey, especially in the energy, tourism, and telecommunication sectors, has also grown visibly in recent years. This has made Turkey cautious about openly criticizing Moscow on some security issues.

Turkey's views on maritime security in the Black Sea area are closer to Russia's than to those of the United States. Ankara essentially

---

[30] John C. K. Daly, "After Crimea: The Future of the Black Sea Fleet," *Jamestown Foundation*, May 22, 2014.

[31] One military option is to provide these countries with their own anti-access capacity; the EU and United States could provide them with ground mobile anti-ship missile and maritime surveillance capabilities.

[32] For a detailed discussion, see F. Stephen Larrabee, "Turkey's New Geopolitics," *Survival*, Vol. 52, No. 2, April–May 2010, pp. 167–169.

regards the Black Sea as a "Turkish lake" and opposes an expansion of both the NATO and the U.S. military presence there. Turkey blocked a U.S. initiative designed to increase the role of NATO's Operation Active Endeavor in the Black Sea in 2006.[33] The NATO initiative conflicted with Operation Black Sea Harmony, an initiative launched by the Turkish Navy in March 2004.

In addition, Turkey feared that an increased U.S. or NATO military presence in the Black Sea could exacerbate tensions with Russia. Turkish officials argue that Black Sea security should be provided by the littoral countries of the Black Sea. Instead of increasing the U.S. or NATO military presence, Turkey proposed expanding the Black Sea Naval Cooperation Task Force (known as BLACKSEAFOR), a multinational naval task force that includes Russia, Ukraine, Georgia, Romania, and Bulgaria.[34]

Turkey also worried that NATO initiatives could lead to the erosion of the 1936 Montreux Convention, which regulates access to the Bosporus and Dardanelles. The convention is a cornerstone of Turkish foreign policy. Ankara is strongly opposed to any initiative that might imply a change in the status of the convention or that could disturb the maritime status quo in the Black Sea region.[35] Thus, any future proposals or initiatives for increased U.S.-Turkish cooperation in the

---

[33] Ümit Enginsoy, and Burak Ege Bekdil, "Turks Oppose U.S. Black Sea Move," *Defense News*, March 13, 2006.

[34] Serkan Demirtas, "Blackseafor to Be Expanded," *Turkish Daily News* (Istanbul), September 19, 2008.

[35] Turkish sensitivity about strictly abiding by provisions of the Montreux Convention was underscored in August 2008 in the immediate aftermath of the Russian invasion of Georgia. The United States sought to send two U.S. Navy hospital ships, the USNS *Comfort* and the USNS *Mercy*, through the Dardanelles with humanitarian aid for Georgia. Their tonnage, however, exceeded the limits allowed for foreign warships under the Montreux Convention. Turkey let it be known that the ships would not be allowed to pass through the Bosphorus because they violated the Montreux Convention. The United States eventually sent the aid aboard the destroyer USS *McFaul*, the USCGC *Dallas*, and the USS *Mount Whitney*, all of which were well below the tonnage limits allowed under the Montreux Convention. See Ümit Enginsoy and Burak Ege Bekdil, "Turkey Jealously Defends Its Rights on the Black Sea," *Defense News*, September 29, 2008. On the U.S. denial that it wanted a change in the Montreux Convention, see Ümit Enginsoy, "No Change Wanted on Turk Straits Convention," *Turkish Daily News* (Istanbul), August 28, 2008.

Black Sea will need to take into consideration Turkey's acute sensitivity regarding changes in the maritime status quo in the region.

CHAPTER FOUR

Conclusions and Implications for the U.S. Army

Even if the current turbulence in Europe, the Greater Middle East, and East Asia prompts the U.S. Congress to agree with the White House to reverse the spending cuts mandated by the Budget Control Act of 2011 (Pub. L. 112–25), U.S. topline defense spending is likely to remain constrained. Therefore, the U.S. defense leadership will have to devise a strategy that enables it to address the increased demands from NATO to shore up its deterrence and defense posture in Eastern Europe in the face of a revisionist Russia, as well as meet its commitments elsewhere in the world, all without counting on substantial increases in programmed force structure or equipment modernization accounts.

The Ukrainian crisis has a number of important possible implications for the U.S. military in general and the Army in particular. First, the assumption that Europe had become a strategically stable continent and that the United States could shift its attention to other regions, especially Asia and the Middle East, has been overturned. Europe will play a more important role in U.S. national security strategy in the coming decade, not a lesser one.

Second, if the Department of Defense is tasked to help NATO build a much more robust deterrence and defense posture in Eastern Europe, the Army and Air Force will need to revisit planning assumptions that have minimized U.S. military commitments to that region since the end of the Cold War. When added to steady or growing demands for U.S. military deployments and activities elsewhere (e.g., East Asia, the Middle East, Africa), this would all but demand a reappraisal of the balance between the requirements of the defense strategy and the resources available to support it. Put simply, many elements of the joint force are being stretched thin to meet new commitments that were not foreseen even as recently as January 2014, when the Quadrennial Defense Review completed its work and the FY 2015 budget submission went forward.

Third, Russia's military actions in Crimea and in the Ukrainian crisis demonstrated a new model of Russian military thinking, combining traditional instruments of Russian military thought with a new emphasis on surprise, deception, and strategic ambiguity. This approach enables Russia to disguise its real intentions and conduct an "invasion by stealth." In the future, NATO is likely to face a Russian military that relies on approaches and techniques associated with Russia's low-cost annexation of Crimea and the destabilization of eastern Ukraine. Countries such as the Baltic states and Moldova, which are on Russia's periphery and have large ethnic Russian minorities on their soil, could be the targets of this new Russian approach to warfare. Moreover, Russia is willing to use conventional forces to compensate for the operational deficiencies of any more subtle use of violence, as demonstrated during August 2014, when several thousand Regular Russian troops were clandestinely infiltrated into eastern Ukraine to defeat the Ukrainian armed forces with firepower-intensive attacks.

Fourth, while overt Russian military action against East European members of NATO is considerably less likely than the more ambiguous and subtle forms of coercion employed in Crimea and eastern Ukraine, an overt conventional attack cannot be entirely excluded. Put simply, Moscow has demonstrated a willingness to escalate to high levels of military operations if more clandestine and strategic ambiguous means do not produce a strategically satisfactory result. NATO as a whole, and the U.S. Army in particular, must prepare for a wide spectrum of threats in the region, including a very high-firepower conventional conflict like the one Putin used at the end of August 2014 in eastern Ukraine.

Fifth, and following from these, the military challenges for the Joint Forces and the U.S. Army in this more complex European security environment will require the development of creative approaches and perhaps investment strategies. While not a return to the Cold War, this threat pattern may require the development of new concepts of air-land operations that span the spectrum of military operations to both counter unconventional threats like that manifested in Ukraine in 2014 and deter conventional Russian attacks.

As the Army considers options for improving its ability to respond to demands in Europe, several planning and investment issues will have to be addressed. If the main security concerns for the Eastern European NATO nations are posed by irregular threats and attempts by pro-Russian groups to destabilize the region, then a major Army mission could be to help Eastern European militaries and other security forces improve their capabilities to deal with the challenge posed by irregular warfare. At the same time, as noted above, the Army and Air Force would have to be prepared to deal with the full spectrum of conflict, including the extensive use of high-firepower weapons (some equipped with precision munitions) in fairly large-scale combat operations.

The possible contributions of other NATO members could influence what U.S. Army elements are needed in Eastern Europe. This will be a high-level political consideration within NATO. Some members may be willing to contribute various capabilities to assist the Eastern European members. Given the relatively short distances from Germany, Italy, France, and other countries to the Baltic states and Romania, the cost of deploying and maintaining other European forces in the region would probably be significantly lower than the cost of transporting U.S. forces from the United States. However, the key question will be what and how much other NATO members are willing to contribute. Once that issue is resolved, the Army's role will be much easier to determine.

To bolster the full spectrum of defense and deterrence requirements, the United States has a number of options for how to use its Army. First, the Army could develop and deploy very high-performance rapid reaction forces by air into Eastern Europe during a period of strategic tension. Such forces have the advantage of not requiring a significant peacetime U.S. presence. On the other hand, these air-transportable forces have less fighting power and tactical mobility than heavier armored and mechanized forces—a serious deficiency in the event of

Russian military escalation. A critical challenge is when to decide to employ these mobile forces during a strategic crisis.

Second, the equipment of heavy forces could be prepositioned in a fashion similar to the Cold War–era storage sites. These require a timely political decision for the troops to be airlifted to fall in on the prepositioned equipment and move to the threatened area. If these storage sites are too forward deployed in Eastern Europe, they may become vulnerable to Russian preemptive action, including the use of special forces and/or long-range precision munitions.

Finally, active mechanized/armored and armored motorized forces could be forward deployed in Eastern Europe. This is the clearest form of deterrence, with forces fully ready for combat, not unlike the "trip wire" posture of the U.S. forces in Berlin during the Cold War era. Currently, this is the politically most contentious option within Europe. Most East European states would find a significant permanent U.S. military presence reassuring. But many of the major Europe powers, notably Germany and Italy, believe such a decision would be provocative and could escalate the current crisis with Russia into a second Cold War. Given the risks and benefits of these various deployment and employment options, it is likely the U.S. Army and U.S. Air Force posture will be a mix of all three approaches, a balance that may well emerge out of the current Ukraine-Russia crisis.

Given the likelihood that unconventional threats will be a major concern in the next decade or more, and assuming that the U.S. Army will have a still-to-be-determined role in assisting the armies of the eastern members of NATO, it is important that the Army retain the skills and capabilities that are focused on that portion of the spectrum of conflict. Importantly, within the Army today there is recognition that the service faces a multifaceted, complex world that will require a wide variety of capabilities.[1]

If the permanent presence of U.S. Army units in Eastern Europe is determined to be necessary, the Defense Department and the Army would need to decide what mix of units would be appropriate. If the

---

[1]   U.S. Army Training and Doctrine Command, *The Army Operating Concept: Win in a Complex World, 2020–2040*, TRADOC PAM 525-3-1, October 7, 2014.

most important contributions to the Eastern European nations are at the lower end of the spectrum of conflict, then intelligence, surveillance, and reconnaissance (ISR), military police, and light infantry units may be the most appropriate types to deploy to the region. Should the principal concern be that Russia might escalate with high-firepower "conventional" forces, the Army's major contribution will likely be conventional formations (e.g., brigade combat teams) and a mix of air and missile defense units to support them, along with other NATO Europe forces. Planners will need guidance to determine the right mix of forces to deploy during peacetime and reinforce during a future strategic crisis.

The greater the expectation that U.S. Army elements might have to fight alongside the much smaller armies of NATO's eastern flank, the greater would be the need for considerable training with them for combined operations. In the unlikely event of an overt "conventional" Russian provocation, many East European NATO armies would be dependent on the United States for such capabilities as fire support and enablers, and perhaps ground maneuver units to defend them. Today, there is relatively little interaction between the U.S. Army and the militaries in Eastern Europe. That interaction should be significantly increased as part of a broader strategy to enhance the defense and deterrence posture of Eastern Europe.

During the Cold War, European NATO members were able to provide considerable infrastructure and logistics support to U.S. Army forces based in Europe. Today, the situation is very different, due to the significant reduction of European NATO defense establishments and infrastructure.[2] Should U.S. forces be stationed or regularly exercise in these areas, an assessment of the infrastructure in the region and its ability to support an increased U.S. military presence would be needed. This would include the need to establish a new joint (and possibly combined) headquarters in the region to manage the overall

---

[2] For a comprehensive discussion, see F. Stephen Larrabee, Stuart E. Johnson, John Gordon IV, Peter A. Wilson, Caroline Baxter, Deborah Lai, and Calin Trentkov-Wermuth, *NATO and the Challenges of Austerity*, Santa Monica, Calif.: RAND Corporation, MG-1196-OSD, 2012, p. i.

American effort, should policy decisions make the stationing of large forces there necessary.

An important joint issue is determining the U.S. Air Force requirements that would be needed to adequately support an increased U.S. Army presence in Europe. Conversely, what capabilities might the Army be called on to provide in support of new Air Force posture and operations (e.g., theater missile defense, Short Range Air Defense [SHORADS], logistical support)? Although the Russian Armed Forces is much smaller than the Soviet-era Red Army, it will likely be equipped with a wide range of long-range precision strike missile systems. If a future crisis began with the use of more subtle and clandestine military violence but then escalated into a regional European war, NATO would face the prospect of long-range precision attacks at the tactical, operational, and strategic level, particularly if Moscow decides to leave the INF treaty and develops long-range cruise and ballistic missiles.

In conclusion, the U.S. Army needs to assess the likely requirements in support of a U.S. national security strategy that is undergoing dynamic change in the face of immediate and likely enduring military challenges that have rapidly emerged in Eastern Europe. Given the constraints on Army force structure and modernization budgets in the coming decade, choices about what forces to commit to Eastern Europe will be difficult. Furthermore, much is still uncertain about a possible increased NATO and/or American military commitment to Eastern Europe. However, this reinforces the importance of developing an array of options and carefully examining their military and political implications.

Finally, it is important to note that several of the considerations put forward in this report, such as increasing the U.S. military's posture in Europe, involve political risks that are beyond the scope of this document to address. Furthermore, and for similar reasons, we offer no judgment on the wisdom of increased investments in defense to address the increased uncertainty and risk in Europe in the context of the overall U.S. fiscal situation. Rather, we note that the status quo that existed when the most recent defense strategy documents were produced has changed and that a reexamination of commitments, both in terms of forces in Europe and defense outlays, is in order.

Bibliography

Aslund, Anders, "Ukraine's Old Internal Enemy," *Wall Street Journal*, October 1, 2014.

Boy, Doritt, "Jazenjuks Kehrtwende," *Frankfurter Allgemeine Zeitung*, August 1, 2014.

Brzezinski, Zbigniew, *The Grand Chessboard*, New York: Basic Books, 1997.

Buchan, David, and David White, "NATO Signs Charter with Ukraine," *Financial Times,* July 10, 1997.

"Charter on a Distinctive Partnership Between the North Atlantic Treaty Organization and Ukraine," *NATO Review,* Vol. 45, No. 4, July–August 1997.

Daly, John C. K., "After Crimea: The Future of the Black Sea Fleet," Jamestown Foundation, May 22, 2014. As of January 8, 2015:
http://www.jamestown.org/programs/tm/single/?tx_ttnews[tt_news]=42411&chas h=bac019ee21bc092c444e87f58808a694

Davis, Julie Hirschfeld, "Obama in Estonia, Calls Ukraine Conflict 'a Moment of Truth,'" *New York Times*, September 3, 2014.

Davis, Paul K., and Peter A. Wilson, *Looming Discontinuities in U.S. Military Strategy and Defense Planning—Colliding RMAs Necessitate a New Strategy*, Santa Monica, Calif.: RAND Corporation, OP-326, 2011. As of November 18, 2014:
http://www.rand.org/pubs/occasional_papers/OP326.html

De Young, Karen, "U.S.: Plane Was Downed from Rebel-Held Area," *Washington Post*, July 19, 2014.

Demirjian, Karoun, and Michael Birnbaum, "Ukraine Accuses Russia of an Incursion," *Washington Post*, November 8, 2014.

Demirtas, Serkan, "Blackseafor to Be Expanded," *Turkish Daily News* (Istanbul), September 19, 2008.

Eddy, Melissa, and Alison Smale, "Under Pact, Russians to Give Gas to Ukraine," *New York Times*, September 27, 2014.

Enginsoy, Ümit, "No Change Wanted on Turk Straits Convention," *Turkish Daily News* (Istanbul), August 28, 2008.

Enginsoy, Ümit, and Burak Ege Bekdil, "Turks Oppose U.S. Black Sea Move," *Defense News*, March 13, 2006.

———, "Turkey Jealously Defends Its Rights on the Black Sea," *Defense News*, September 29, 2008.

Erlanger, Stephen, Julie Herschfeld Davis, and Stephen Castle, "NATO Plans a Special Force to Reassure Eastern Europe and Deter Russia," *New York Times*, September 6, 2014.

Ewing, Jack, and Gala Pianigiana, "Slowdown in Italy Adds to Fears Over Ukraine," *New York Times International*, August 7, 2014.

Faiola, Anthony, "Ukraine's President Offers Deal to the Separatists as Truce Frays," *Washington Post*, September 16, 2014.

Gauck, Joachim, "Germany's Role in the World: Reflections on Responsibility, Norms and Alliances," speech at the Opening of the Munich Security Conference, January 31, 2014.

Giles, Chris, and Stefan Wagstyl, "IMF Warns of Third Eurozone Recession Since Financial Crisis," *Financial Times*, October 8, 2014.

Gordon, Michael R., Andrew E. Kramer, and Eric Schmitt, "Putin Is Said to Expand Forces Near Ukraine," *New York Times International*, August 5, 2014.

Gordon, Michael R., and Andrew E. Kramer, "Russia Continues to Train and Equip Ukrainian Rebels, NATO Official Says," *New York Times*, November 4, 2014.

Guriev, Sergei, "Russia Can't Withstand Lower Oil Prices Forever," *Financial Times*, October 20, 2014.

Gustafson, Thane, "Russia May Pivot to the East But It Cannot Escape Its European Destiny," *Financial Times*, November 20, 2014.

Hamilton, Daniel S., Andras Simonyi, and Debra L. Cagan, eds., *Advancing U.S.-Nordic-Baltic Security Cooperation*, Washington D.C.: Center for Transatlantic Relations, 2014.

Herszenhorn, David M., "Fall in Oil Prices Poses a Problem for Russia, Iraq and Others," *New York Times*, October 16, 2014.

Higgins, Andrew, "Tensions Surge in Estonia Amid a Russian Replay of the Cold War," *New York Times*, October 6, 2014.

Hille, Kathrin, "Russia to Curb Defense Spending," *Financial Times*, October 13, 2014.

"Importverbot trifft russische Mittelschickt," *Frankfurter Allgemeine Zeitung*, August 11, 2014.

Jones, Claire, "Russian Tensions Hit Fragile Eurozone Growth," *Financial Times*, August 11, 2014.

Larrabee, F. Stephen, "Ukraine at the Crossroads," *Washington Quarterly*, Fall 2007.

————, "Turkey's New Geopolitics," *Survival*, Vol. 52, No. 2, April–May 2010.

Larrabee, F. Stephen, Stuart E. Johnson, John Gordon IV, Peter A. Wilson, Caroline Baxter, Deborah Lai, and Calin Trentkov-Wermuth, *NATO and the Challenges of Austerity*, Santa Monica, Calif.: RAND Corporation, MG-1196-OSD, 2012. As of November 18, 2014:
http://www.rand.org/pubs/monographs/MG1196.html

Larson, Jeffrey A., "The Wales Summit and NATO's Deterrence Capabilities: An Assessment," NDC Research Report, NATO Defense College, November 2014.

MacFarqhuar, Neal, "Aid Elusive, Crimea Farms Face Hurdles," *New York Times*, July 8, 2014.

McLees, Alexandra, and Eugene Rumer, "Saving Ukraine's Defense Industry," Carnegie Endowment for Peace, July 30, 2014.

"MH-17 Crash: Investigation Focuses on '25 Metal Shards,'" *BBC News Europe*, September 12, 2014.

Michta, Andrew, "Putin Targets the Scandinavians," *The American Interest*, November 17, 2014. As of January 8, 2015:
http://www.the-american-interest.com/2014/11/17/
putin-targets-the-scandinavians/

Milne, Richard, Sam Jones, and Kathrin Hille, "Russian Air Incursions Rattle Baltic States," *Financial Times*, September 25, 2014.

Norberg, Johan, and Fredrik Westerlund, "Russia and Ukraine: Military-Strategic Options, and Possible Risks, for Moscow," The International Institute for Strategic Studies, April 7, 2014.

Official Site of the President of Russia, "Meeting of the Valdai International Discussion Club," October 24, 2014. As of January 8, 2015:
http://eng.news.kremlin.ru/news/23137/print

Olearchyk, Roman, and Neil Buckley, "Russian Stealth Forced Ukraine into a Ceasefire," *Financial Times*, September 14, 2014.

Oliver, Christian, Jack Farchy, and Roman Olearchyk, "Moscow and Kiev Reach Deal on Gas Flows," *Financial Times*, October 31, 2014.

Peel, Quentin, "Merkel Wants a Stable World and Is Willing to Pay a Price," *Financial Times*, August 12, 2014.

Pifer, Steven, "Taking Stock in Ukraine," *The American Interest*, October 28, 2014. As of January 8, 2015:
http://www.the-american-interest.com/articles/2014/10/28

"Putin Is Leading Russia Down an Isolationist Path," *Financial Times*, October 8, 2014.

"Putin schockt die Bauern in Osteuropa," *Frankfurter Allgemeine Zeitung*, August 8, 2014.

Putin, Vladimir, prepared remarks before the 43rd Munich Conference on Security, Munich, Germany, February 12, 2007.

"Putin's Reach: Merkel Concerned About Russian Influence in the Balkans," *Der Spiegel*, November 17, 2014. As of January 8, 2015:
http://www.spiegel.de/international/europe/germany-worried-about-russian-influence-in-the-balkans-a-1003427.html

Sattar, Majid, "Schlussetappe auf dem langen Weg nach Westen," *Frankfurter Allgemeine Zeitung*, August 26, 2014.

Speck, Ulrich, "How the EU Sleepwalked into a Conflict with Russia," Carnegie Europe, July 10, 2014. As of October 28, 2014:
http://carnegieeurope.eu/2014/07/10/how-eu-sleepwalked-into-conflict-with-russia

Spiegel, Peter, "Putin Demands Reopening of EU Trade Pact with Ukraine," *Financial Times*, September 26, 2014.

Steinmeier, Frank-Walter, Foreign Minister, speech at the 50th Munich Security Conference, January 31, 2014.

Sutyagin, Igor, "Russia's Overestimated Military Might," *RUSI Newsbrief*, March 25, 2014.

Sutyagin, Igor, and Michael Clarke, "Ukraine Military Dispositions—the Military Ticks Up While the Clock Ticks Down," *RUSI Briefing Paper*, April 2014.

U.S. Army Training and Doctrine Command, *The Army Operating Concept: Win in a Complex World, 2020–2040*, TRADOC PAM 525-3-1, October 7, 2014.

Vendil Pallin, Carolina, ed., *Russian Military Capability in a Ten-Year Perspective—2011*, Stockholm: Swedish Ministry of Defense, 2012.

von der Leyen, Ursula, speech at the 50th Munich Security Conference, January 31, 2014.

Wagstyl, Stefan, "Merkel Rethink on Tough Action Reflects Loss of Trust in Putin," *Financial Times*, July 31, 2014.